THE HISTORY OF THE ST. LOUIS RAMS

Published by Creative Education
123 South Broad Street
Mankato, Minnesota 56001
Creative Education is an imprint of The Creative Company.

DESIGN AND PRODUCTION BY **EVANSDAY DESIGN**

LIBRARY OF CONGRESS CATALOGING-IN-PUBLICATION DATA

Bell, Lonnie.
The history of the St. Louis Rams / by Lonnie Bell.
p. cm. — (NFL today)
Summary: Traces the history of the team from its beginnings
through 2003.
ISBN 978-1-58341-311-1
1. St. Louis Rams (Football team)—History—Juvenile literature.
[1. St. Louis Rams (Football team)—History. 2. Football—History.]
I. Title. II. Series.

GV956.S85B45 2004
796.332'64'0977866—dc22   2003062575

9 8 7 6 5 4 3

COVER PHOTO: wide receiver Torry Holt

RAMS

ST. LOUIS, MISSOURI, WAS FOUNDED IN 1764, JUST DOWNSTREAM FROM THE POINT WHERE THE MISSISSIPPI AND MISSOURI RIVERS MEET. EARLY PIONEERS USED THE FRONTIER TOWN AS AN ENTRY POINT, OR "GATEWAY," TO THE WEST. BECAUSE OF THIS, ST. LOUIS WAS NICKNAMED THE "GATEWAY CITY." TODAY, COUNTLESS VISITORS HEADING WEST STILL STOP IN ST. LOUIS, OFTEN TO VISIT THE FAMOUS GATEWAY ARCH, WHICH TOWERS 630 FEET INTO THE SKY. IN 1995, ST. LOUIS BECAME THE HOME OF A NATIONAL FOOTBALL LEAGUE (NFL) TEAM CALLED THE RAMS. LIKE THE EARLY PIONEERS WHO TREKKED THROUGH THE CITY, THE RAMS HAD A RESTLESS HISTORY. WHEN THE TEAM FIRST JOINED THE NFL IN 1937, IT WAS LOCATED IN CLEVELAND, OHIO. THE RAMS HEADED WEST TO LOS ANGELES IN 1946. FINALLY, IN 1995, THE TEAM MOVED BACK EAST TO ST. LOUIS, WHERE IT HAS BEEN BUTTING HEADS WITH NFL OPPONENTS EVER SINCE.

THE CLEVELAND YEARS>

BETWEEN 1937 AND 1944, the Cleveland Rams had a hard time living up to their feisty name. The team had some exciting players, including quarterback Parker Hall and running back Johnny "Zero" Drake. But by 1945, the Rams had yet to put together a winning record. Fan support was low, and team owner Dan Reeves decided to relocate to Los Angeles. But before they moved, the Rams spent one more year in Cleveland—and what a year it was.

Quarterback Bob Waterfield signed with Cleveland in 1945 and quickly earned the nickname "the Rifle" because of his strong arm and pinpoint passing to star end Jim Benton. Late in the season, the 7–1 Rams needed just one victory to claim the NFL Western Division title.

But Waterfield was suffering from a rib injury. In the locker room before the next game, a trainer told Rams coach Adam Walsh that he couldn't use the quarterback. "The heck you can't!" Waterfield exploded. "Tape me up and give me a shot!"

His chest wrapped in tape, Waterfield took the field, passed for more than 300 yards, and led the Rams to a 38–21 victory over the Detroit Lions. As Western Division champs, the Rams then hosted the Washington Redskins in the NFL championship game. On game day, the temperature was below freezing, with an icy wind whipping across the field. The weather didn't faze Waterfield, though. Throwing, running, and kicking the ball, he led the Rams to a 15–14 win and their first world championship. When he was named the NFL's Most Valuable Player (MVP), Cleveland fans roared their approval. Then, the team headed west.

Down! Silver 9 Set! Hut Hut!

A CALIFORNIA CHAMPIONSHIP>

LOS ANGELES FANS embraced their new team, and the Rams rewarded them by finishing 6–4–1 in 1946. The Rams also made football history in their first year in California by signing running back Kenny Washington and end Woody Strode—the first African-American players in the NFL.

Over the next few years, Los Angeles became one of the most exciting offensive teams in the league. The Rams already featured Benton, and in 1948, they drafted another sensational receiver named Tom Fears. With Waterfield leading this talent, no opponent's lead seemed safe. In one 1948 game, the Rams fell behind the Philadelphia Eagles 28–0 before Waterfield led them back to a 28–28 tie.

The Rams' air attack became even deadlier in 1949, when the team drafted a speedy running back and receiver named Elroy "Crazylegs" Hirsch. With Hirsch zipping around the field catching Waterfield's passes, the Rams went 8–2–2 in 1949 and won the Western Division title. Unfortunately, they lost to the Philadelphia Eagles in the NFL championship game, 14–0.

Los Angeles was the NFL's highest-scoring team in 1950 and 1951. In 1950, the Rams set a new league record with 466 total points, scoring 70 of them in a single game. During those seasons, Waterfield split playing time with a young quarterback named Norm Van Brocklin. When Van Brocklin emerged as the team's leading passer, fans wondered if Waterfield would be traded. Team owner Dan Reeves, however, scoffed at the idea. "I wouldn't trade Bob for the Brooklyn Bridge, with any player you name thrown in."

The high-powered Rams won the Western Division in both 1950 and 1951. In 1950, they lost to the Cleveland Browns in the NFL championship game, 30–28. But in 1951, the Rams refused to lose. In that game, Waterfield led the Rams to a 14–0 lead over the Browns. Then, with three minutes left, Van Brocklin threw a 73-yard touchdown pass to Fears to seal a 24–17 win and the Rams' second NFL title.

Receiving/pass receiver Elroy Hirsch scored 17 touchdowns in 1951, each covering an average of 41 yards.

Los Angeles fans were overjoyed by the championship. But after Waterfield retired in 1952, the Rams lost their grip on the top spot in the Western Division. The team still had plenty of offensive talent, as well as rugged defensive end Andy Robustelli. But with the exception of an 8–3–1 season in 1955, the Rams put together mediocre seasons during the rest of the '50s.

A star of the 1960s, defensive end Deacon Jones is credited with originating the term "quarterback sack."

GABRIEL AND A FEARSOME FOURSOME>

AFTER VAN BROCKLIN left town in 1957, Rams offi-

cials searched far and wide for another star quarterback.

In 1962, they found him by drafting Roman Gabriel. With

Gabriel at the helm in 1966, the Rams posted their first

winning record (8–6) in eight years. Offensively, the

Rams were powered by Gabriel and running back Dick

Bass. Defensively, linemen Rosey Grier, Merlin Olsen,

Deacon Jones, and Lamar Lundy—a dominant quartet

known as the "Fearsome Foursome"—thrilled fans and

throttled opposing quarterbacks. "Until we came along,"

Olsen said, "most fans only looked to offensive players

for excitement. The emergence of our line brought some

attention over to the defense."

Roman Gabriel threw 154 touchdown passes for Los Angeles, a total that remains the franchise record.

Lawrence McCutcheon had four 1,000-yard seasons

Merlin Olsen made the Pro Bowl for 14 straight years

In 1967, 1968, and 1969, the Rams posted a combined 32–7–3 record and won the National Football Conference (NFC) Western Division twice. Unfortunately, they made quick exits from the play-offs both times, losing to the Green Bay Packers in 1967 and the Minnesota Vikings in 1969. Still, fans cheered when Gabriel was named NFL MVP after the 1969 season. The quarterback was quick to give credit to his teammates. "I'm a successful quarterback because I'm on a successful team," Gabriel said modestly.

The Rams remained a powerhouse in the 1970s, winning the NFC West every year from 1973 to 1979. But despite the addition of such talented players as linebacker Isiah Robertson, defensive end Jack Youngblood, and running back Lawrence McCutcheon, the team could never quite reach the Super Bowl—that is, not until 1979. That year, the Rams went just 9–7 but then won two playoff games to reach the Super Bowl, where they faced the mighty Pittsburgh Steelers. Los Angeles led 19–17 after three quarters, but the Steelers came back to win 31–19. Soon after that, many of the Rams' stars of the '70s retired or moved on.

FROM DICKERSON TO EVERETT>

DURING A STRIKE-SHORTENED 1982 season, the

Rams finished last in the NFC West with a 2–7 record.

To turn things around, Los Angeles then brought in a

new coach and a new star. The coach was John Robinson,

who had been a successful college coach at the nearby

University of Southern California. The star was young

running back Eric Dickerson, acquired with the second

pick in the 1983 NFL Draft.

During training camp in 1983, Coach Robinson thought

Dickerson was being lazy and yelled at the rookie to work

harder. Robinson finally realized that Dickerson was work-

ing hard; he was just so naturally talented that he made

everything look effortless. "He made no noise when he

ran," Robinson recalled. "If you were blind, he could run

right by you, and I don't think you'd know he was there

unless you felt the wind."

Eric Dickerson's 2,105 rushing yards in 1984 are one of the most impressive records in all of sports.

A consistently brilliant receiver, Henry Ellard led Los Angeles in catches from 1984 to 1992.

Dickerson left plenty of defenders in his wind in the mid-1980s. As a rookie, he shocked the sports world by rushing for 1,808 yards. In 1984, he charged for an incredible 2,105 yards—an NFL record that still stands. Behind Dickerson's super-human efforts and a stout defense that featured linebacker Jim Collins, the Rams made the playoffs every year from 1983 to 1986. Unfortunately, the team's passing attack was weak, and Los Angeles lost in the playoffs every time.

Although Dickerson was traded away after the 1987 season, new quarterback Jim Everett kept the Rams on the winning track. In 1988, Everett threw an NFL-best 31 touchdown passes, many of them to star receiver Henry Ellard. In 1989, Everett and Ellard led Los Angeles to an 11–5 record and an appearance in the NFC championship game. Sadly, the Super Bowl remained just out of reach, as the San Francisco 49ers crushed the Rams 30–3.

THE 1989 SEASON turned out to be the last hurrah for the Los Angeles Rams, who slipped to the bottom of the NFC West standings. The team featured some exciting players in the early 1990s, including linebacker Kevin Greene and bruising running back Jerome Bettis. But by 1994, the team had suffered five straight losing seasons, and fan support was dwindling. Before the 1995 season, team owner Georgia Frontiere decided to give the Rams a new start in St. Louis.

More than 60,000 St. Louis fans packed into Busch Stadium to welcome their new team on opening day in 1995. The Rams, who were used to playing in a near-empty stadium in Los Angeles, seemed energized by the crowd and upset the Green Bay Packers 17–14. "The environment is so much more positive for our team," said the team's head coach, Rich Brooks. "It's what we really needed."

A rugged 250-pounder with speed, rookie rusher Jerome Bettis rumbled for 1,429 yards in 1993.

After that opening win, the Rams struggled in their first few seasons in St. Louis. But in the late '90s, the team quietly stockpiled talent. In 1997, former Philadelphia Eagles coach Dick Vermeil was hired as head coach. In 1999, the Rams traded several draft picks to the Indianapolis Colts for swift running back Marshall Faulk. That year, the team also drafted a speedy receiver named Torry Holt to line up alongside star receiver Isaac Bruce.

Of these additions, it was Faulk who excited fans the most. A remarkable athlete, Faulk had played as a quarterback, running back, end, wide receiver, and defensive player in high school. During his NFL career in Indianapolis, he had run for more than 1,000 yards in four seasons. "What sets him apart from everybody else," said former Indianapolis coach Ted Marchibroda, "is that he can go from a standing start to full speed faster than anybody I've ever seen."

THE GREATEST SHOW ON TURF >

THE 1999 SEASON was a magical one in St. Louis. After going 4–12 the year before, the Rams soared to a 13–3 record and the NFC championship. Helping make this miraculous turnaround possible was quarterback Kurt Warner. Only a few years earlier, Warner—unable to catch on with any NFL team—had worked in an Iowa grocery store. But when the Rams' starting quarterback was injured before the 1999 season, Warner stepped in and astounded fans by throwing for 41 touchdowns. "I told our team we could win with Kurt," said Coach Vermeil. "I didn't expect that we'd win *because* of him."

In the playoffs, the high-scoring Rams beat the Minnesota Vikings and Tampa Bay Buccaneers to advance to the Super Bowl, where they faced the Tennessee Titans. The game was tied 16–16 late in the fourth quarter when Warner fired a 74-yard touchdown strike to Isaac Bruce.

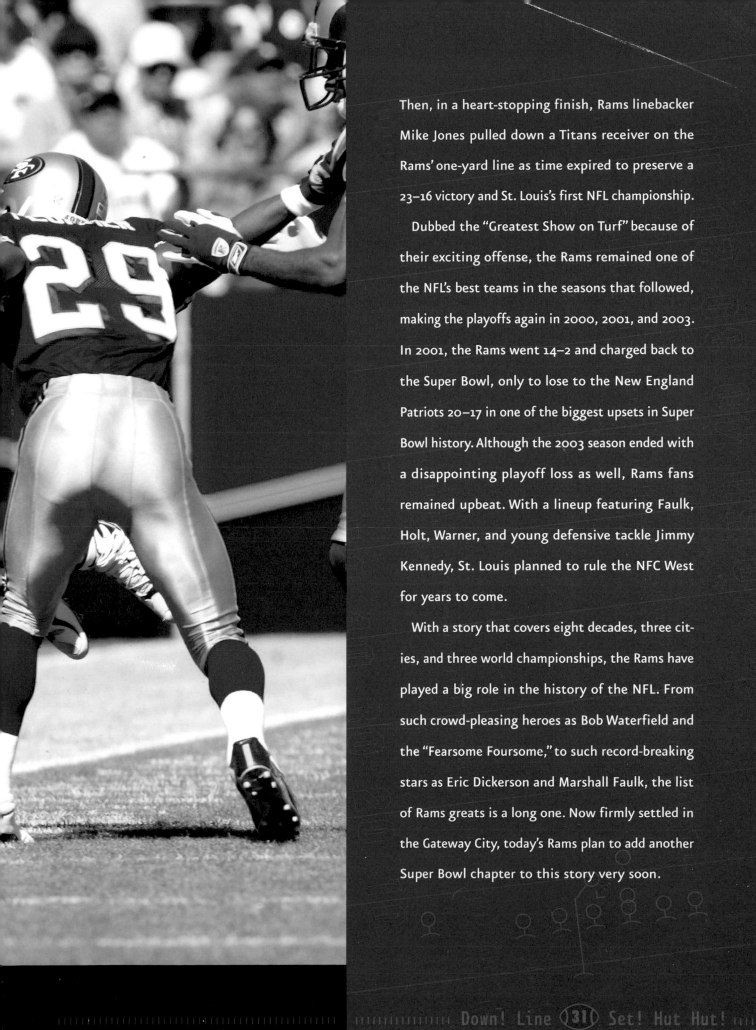

Then, in a heart-stopping finish, Rams linebacker Mike Jones pulled down a Titans receiver on the Rams' one-yard line as time expired to preserve a 23–16 victory and St. Louis's first NFL championship.

Dubbed the "Greatest Show on Turf" because of their exciting offense, the Rams remained one of the NFL's best teams in the seasons that followed, making the playoffs again in 2000, 2001, and 2003. In 2001, the Rams went 14–2 and charged back to the Super Bowl, only to lose to the New England Patriots 20–17 in one of the biggest upsets in Super Bowl history. Although the 2003 season ended with a disappointing playoff loss as well, Rams fans remained upbeat. With a lineup featuring Faulk, Holt, Warner, and young defensive tackle Jimmy Kennedy, St. Louis planned to rule the NFC West for years to come.

With a story that covers eight decades, three cities, and three world championships, the Rams have played a big role in the history of the NFL. From such crowd-pleasing heroes as Bob Waterfield and the "Fearsome Foursome," to such record-breaking stars as Eric Dickerson and Marshall Faulk, the list of Rams greats is a long one. Now firmly settled in the Gateway City, today's Rams plan to add another Super Bowl chapter to this story very soon.

INDEX>